ECONOMIC DEVELOPMENT IS NOT FOR AMATEURS!

A must-read for community leaders on how to achieve economic development success

BY

JAY GARNER & ROSS PATTEN

Economic Development Is Not for Amateurs! A must-read for community leaders on how to achieve economic development success

Copyright © 2020 Jay Garner and Ross Patten

ISBN 13: 9798666846582

First Edition

Printed in the United States of America

Preface

Having served in the economic development profession for more than 40 years, I've seen one common denominator related to a community's economic development success: leadership. The quality of a community's public and private leadership drives success. Excellent leadership brings economic prosperity to a community, region, or state. Poor leadership drives economic activity out of that location.

Many small and mid-sized communities throughout the country face a multitude of challenges to convince residents and businesses to reinvest in their community. Faced with rising commercial vacancies and challenging socioeconomic realities, once-thriving business districts that were the heartbeat of their community now appear rundown and blighted. Unfortunately, government budgets are increasingly tight, and there are limited resources to help reverse these trends. This is especially true in a post-COVID-19 world. Furthermore, while newly elected policymakers are eager to support businesses and job creation efforts, most are not well-versed in "Economic Development 101" and wonder where to start.

My book partner, Ross Patten and I wrote this book to help policymakers (elected officials), board directors for economic development organizations and chambers of commerce, community or state leaders, and officials and volunteers in leadership capacities successfully navigate the complexities of economic development. Too many people make economic development success challenging. It doesn't need to be. It's not rocket science. But it is an art with plenty of technicalities associated with its successful implementation. This book breaks down the complexities for the reader to comprehend.

Our guidance will help leaders hit the ground running by modeling strategy, tactics, and best practices from across the nation and help plan your future success. Enjoy the ride!

Jay Garner

Jay and I are passionate about helping communities grow, invest in themselves, and sometimes simply get out of their own way! In this book, we start with high-level changes that can be implemented at the state or regional level to set the stage for local success, then we make our way into the weeds with specific recommendations that local communities can model to create big changes. Whether you represent a big or small constituency, it's important to see the whole picture so you can make changes to what you can control and then advocate for changes to the elements you don't control.

Importantly, Jay and I do not come from the same geography, life experience, generation, or ideology. While our ideas and perspectives sometimes differ, our goals as practitioners are always the same — to create opportunity and wealth within our communities. These are politically divisive times, but every community wants good jobs, opportunities, and strong neighborhoods. From day one, use economic development as the unifying force in your community to unite diverse stakeholders and get good projects done.

Ross Patten

TABLE OF CONTENTS

CHAPTER 1

*Effective Leadership =
Community Prosperity*

Key Takeaways:

1. The quality of your public and private leadership drives economic development success.

2. Certainty, simplicity, and speed comprise the three tenets of successful communities.

3. Divisiveness kills deals.

4. It's essential to work toward effectively training and enhancing your community servants to be effective leaders.

5. Economic development is defined as what leaders need to do to enhance wealth-

building opportunities for their constituents and build a quality of place that attracts and retains residents and visitors.

Leadership is the common denominator for all economic development success.

Having spent 40 years doing economic development work around the country, which included observing the winners and losers of states, regions, and municipal jurisdictions related to achieving economic development success (wealth-building for the citizens of those jurisdictions), I've learned a universal truth. The common denominator of a community's success is *always* the quality of your public and private leadership. Excellent leadership drives economic development to your community. Poor leadership drives economic development out. It is as simple as that.

What do successful communities have in common that allow them to beat the competition? In short, it's certainty, simplicity, and speed. In this global economy, "speed to market" is a buzz phrase that has meaning. It defines the ability for the private sector to be up and operational in the least amount of time possible so businesses can make a profit and operate successfully. Governments are a key factor in determining how effective speed to market can actually be. So, this is where certainty, simplicity, and speed are of paramount importance. Is there certainty with the permitting and regulatory process? Will a government bureaucrat interpret code on his or her whim rather than following the rules? Will the process take days, weeks, or months? Let's be very clear: months are a deal killer. And, the fewer the weeks the better. Does the government jurisdiction have customer-friendly processes that define simplicity, such as a one-stop permitting shop? All of these components help define the three tenets of **certainty, simplicity, and speed**. Use that as your mantra in the jurisdiction you represent whether your role is an elected policymaker or a government official whose responsibility it is to implement policy.

But much more than the permitting and regulatory process drive economic development success emanating from leadership. Successful communities have these attributes in common:

- **A vision.** Is there a community strategy or a common vision to achieve economic development success? There needs to be. With a vision that becomes an actionable plan, you have direction. Without a vision or plan, you're rudderless. The keyword here is *actionable*.

Stay away from consultants that want to give you a 30,000-foot view or pie-in-the-sky recommendations. It's important to be innovative and creative in your strategic action plans, but at the end of the day, they need to be pragmatic and implementable.

- **A desire to achieve success.** No community will ever have unanimity in having a unified vision or plan, but there is a need to attempt to reach consensus. With consensus, there is usually a desire to achieve common economic development goals. With that desire, the plan and the tools to achieve success can be obtained. A case in point is the state of Texas. In 1979, the state legislature decentralized economic development by allowing communities in Texas to control their own destiny by allowing by popular vote, a half-cent sales tax for economic development. It is in the state's constitution, and today it's called Type A and Type B sales tax, the latter offering more options to create product within municipalities, such as museums, art centers, amateur and professional sports facilities, and much more.[1]

---

[1] "Type A and B economic development corporations overview," Texas Comptroller of Public Accounts, accessed July, 11, 2020, https://comptroller.texas.gov/economy/local/type-ab/.

This has been the game-changer in Texas and is a key factor in Texas leading the nation in job growth for the last 16 years. In the next chapter, you will read about a related mantra we use: *No product, No project™*. With this half-cent sales tax, municipalities in Texas were able to create product such as industrial and office parks. With product, came jobs. None of this would have happened without the leadership and vision of a particular Texas legislator who served as the champion, and then the culmination of the entire legislature to adopt it. Was it difficult? Absolutely. No one (or mostly no one) likes taxes. Was it effective? The results speak for themselves.

- **A desire to unite for the good of the community.** Divisiveness kills deals. Case in point: Amazon's second headquarters (HQ2) announcement in Queens borough, New York, in 2018. Over 200 communities in North America submitted applications to be considered for Amazon's second and third headquarters. Many of them did not even qualify, but they submitted anyway and spent lots of money in doing so. The one positive about this very public search process is that it brought many communities together (internally) to unite for a common good. These communities wanted that project, the 25,000 jobs, and the billions in capital investment associated with the project. Except for one — Queens in New York City. The pushback by community activists (most of which was unfounded or ill-informed) was so exorbitant and caustic that Amazon withdrew its announcement several weeks after it was made. Mind you, I probably would not have Queens (or New York City) on my list in the first place because of a challenging business environment and, as Amazon soon found out, an environment that's not conducive to achieving success. Conversely, northern Virginia rolled out the red carpet for Amazon as the other possible HQ2 location and was rewarded by winning the project. And then, unexpectedly, Amazon announced at nearly the same time, an operations center in Nashville with 5,000 employees unrelated to the HQ2 project, but still a significant win. A ticker-tape parade would have been offered by the economic development leaders in Tennessee and Nashville if Amazon requested it. So, yes, divisiveness kills projects.

- **Create and maintain infrastructure.** This seems so basic and simple, but it often gets overlooked by policymakers. Funding must be kept up to build and maintain roads, water and sewer infrastructure, broadband, public safety, housing stock, and more. When communities fund infrastructure, they're investing in the people of that community for today and building a future for its citizens of tomorrow. When they don't, investment leaves the community.

- **Build the talent pipeline.** Another mantra you will read about in a subsequent chapter is having a labor force that is work ready. Communities must invest in themselves to build the talent pipeline. This is done by offering career academies or career pathways in secondary schools, having higher education options that include community colleges and technical schools, offering customized training options for employers, having a quality of place that will attract new residents since more people in a community means a stable workforce, and offering training opportunities for people to skill themselves up with the tools they need to succeed in an increasingly automated world.

How do you build this leadership pipeline? How are leaders created? I subscribe to the idea that people are taught leadership; they're not necessarily born as leaders. You may need a role model to learn from to build the characteristics that leaders demonstrate. Effective leadership traits include courage, passion, confidence, commitment, and ambition.[2] There are programs and learning initiatives that help shape and define leaders that serve in a public role. One good example of this effort is the Georgia Academy for Economic Development.[3] The academy was started in 1993 by a consortium of public and private organizations involved in economic development. The program is designed to enhance community leaders' skills and knowledge so that more communities in Georgia may remain or become successful. More than 6,500 Georgians have graduated from this program, which is supported by over 20 statewide organizations, with facilitators, coordinators, and program management provided by Georgia Electric

---

[2] "8 Must-Have Qualities of an Effective Leader," Michael Page, accessed July, 11, 2020,
https://www.michaelpage.com/advice/management-advice/development-and-retention/8-must-have-qualities-effective-leader.
[3] "Georgia Department of Community Affairs," Georgia, accessed July, 11, 2020,
https://www.dca.ga.gov/local-government-assistance/partnerships/georgia-academy-economic-development.

Membership Corporation, Georgia Power, and the Georgia Department of Community Affairs.

So how's it going to be? Lead, follow, or get out of the way? As a leader, lead. Make no apologies. Sure, you'll make some people angry. As a public servant, you'll run into more than your share of CAVE people (citizens against virtually everything) and the NIMBYs (not in my backyard), but being a leader and doing the right thing will have a profound impact on the constituents you serve and can be rewarding beyond measure. I've had more than one effective public servant tell me that the reason for his or her success was because they made decisions as if they weren't running again. They focused on what was in the best interest for their communities or constituents in the long term. Strong leadership drives the means to achieve the end goal — quality job creation and investment within your states, regions, and communities. With effective leadership and your ability to instill passion and confidence in others, good things will happen in your community!

CHAPTER 2

No Product, No Project™

Key Takeaways:

1. *No product, No project*™. You can't sell from an empty wagon.

2. Speed to market is important since 85% of all project searches start by looking for an existing building.

3. Spec buildings are a plus to attract prospect activity. But with a risk.

4. Creating a long-term, sustainable funding source for economic development.

infrastructure (product) is a recipe for success.

No product, No project™. It's really as simple as that. You just can't sell from an empty wagon. If community leaders are serious about job creation and capital investment, then there needs to be "product" that can be marketed and ultimately sold or leased. Without product, a community will be overlooked or passed over by prospective companies for communities that DO have the type of product companies desire. So, what is product?

Product is defined as those tangible real estate assets that either allow businesses to operate or as a necessary resource for that real estate development to succeed (infrastructure). Dirt, without the appropriate infrastructure in place, does not make a site. Real estate product can be industrial, office, and commercial (retail); speculative, build-to-suit and previously occupied buildings. Product can also be the conduits to make these sites and buildings viable and marketable. That includes water and wastewater infrastructure, broadband, gas and electric, transportation infrastructure, and the list goes on. It also includes what some may call soft infrastructure like libraries, parks and recreation facilities, art centers, bike and walking paths, and other investments that enhance the quality of place for your community.

In Chapter 1, we discussed the Texas miracle of the half-cent sales tax for economic development product called Type B sales tax. The rules regarding what you can use these tax funds for are generous and allow for the construction and development of a litany of supporting infrastructure projects to help create or support primary jobs.[4] These include:

- Professional and amateur sports and athletic facilities, tourism and entertainment facilities, convention facilities and public parks;

- Related store, restaurant, concession, parking and transportation facilities;

- Related street, water and sewer facilities; and

- Affordable housing.

To promote and develop new and expanded business enterprises that create or retain primary

[4] "Eligible Type B Projects: Developing Industries and Cultivating Communities," Texas Comptroller of Public Accounts, accessed July 11, 2020, https://comptroller.texas.gov/economy/local/type-ab/type-b.php.

jobs, a Type B Economic Development Corporation (EDC) may fund:

- Public safety facilities;
- Recycling facilities;
- Streets, roads, drainage, and related improvements;
- Demolition of existing structures;
- General municipally owned improvements; and
- Maintenance and operating costs associated with projects.

State policy can be a great way to build product. Only a few states have some semblance of a similar effort to the Texas model including, Georgia and West Virginia, which have enacted local option sales taxes for economic development purposes. That said, Ohio has a very aggressive and entrepreneurial effort called JobsOhio that funds its economic development effort and in many cases, product related to economic development through grants.[5] JobsOhio's funding model is unlike the

---

[5] "Understanding JobsOhio's Funding," JobsOhio, accessed July 11, 2020, https://www.jobsohio.com/about-jobsohio/about-us/understanding-jobsohios-funding/.

funding model for any other economic development organization in the country in that no tax dollars or other public dollars are used to support it. JobsOhio is a private nonprofit corporation wholly funded by an independent private source — the profits from the JobsOhio Beverage System (JOBS) liquor enterprise. These are great state examples to model.

Similarly, local communities need to invest in product development to fit the needs of their community. Though limited in the number of state efforts to develop product, local product development initiative has been replicated by a number of communities around the United States, such as Topeka, Kansas, and Bartlesville and Tulsa, Oklahoma.[6] Projects that qualify in Topeka and Shawnee County, Kansas, include broadband infrastructure, the development of industrial parks, streetscapes, and much more. In Bartlesville, incentives are set aside for qualifying companies for free land and cash incentives (which is a rarity these days). In Tulsa, Oklahoma, the product is centered around the attraction of talent (people)

---

[6] "JEDO Home: Joint Economic Development Organization," JEDO, accessed July 11, 2020, https://www.jedoecodevo.com/; Bartlesville Development Authority, accessed July 11, 2020, http://www.bdaok.org/.

through a program named Tulsa Remote.[7] The program is a unique recruitment initiative aimed at attracting talented individuals to Tulsa. The program brings remote workers and mobile entrepreneurs to the community by providing $10,000 grants and numerous community-building opportunities. Each grant is distributed over the course of a year to eligible remote workers or entrepreneurs living outside of Oklahoma. Funding is currently provided by the George Kaiser Family Foundation. The city of Tulsa and other community organizations lend their support to ensure program participants are fully immersed and engaged in the community.

Why is finding a funding source important in relationship to product? Well, product development takes money and time. You need to have product to market and sell, so using creative tactics to help fund product expenditures is important. We're sympathetic to communities that don't have a lot of money and face tough budget decisions. However, rarely do we work with a community that doesn't face financial struggles. This is where strong leadership is required to get the community to "invest in itself," because the cost is too great not to!

---

[7] Tulsa Remote, accessed July 11, 2020, https://tulsaremote.com/.

It's also as important to control the product. A saying we like to use is, *"The entity that controls the dirt, controls the project."* If the real estate is not government- or quasi public-controlled, then you're at the whim of the private property owner in making the deal happen. This is why you'll see, especially in smaller jurisdictions, municipally owned industrial parks. These parks are designed to not necessarily make a profit for the community, but instead allow for the infrastructure, the product if you will, to be available for businesses to own and or operate. The municipality gets its return from new and retained jobs, new or expanded capital investment, and new taxes on the assessor's ledger. The long-term return on investment is typically far greater than the initial costs of the project.

A speculative (spec) building is another tool that many communities have used to spur economic growth. This is particularly true in smaller communities where private real estate developers are hesitant to take the risk in developing a spec building. Having a spec building in your community is analogous to selling your house. The more people you have come to look at your house, the greater the chance you have in selling it. A spec building works on the same principle. A rule of thumb by site-selection advisory professionals is that approximately 85 percent of all project searches start with a company looking for an existing building. Prior to COVID-19 and the economic calamity it has caused, we were operating in the United States with an especially hot economy, and quality buildings with vacancies were hard to find. Oftentimes, the search would turn into a greenfield project. But, having a spec building in your inventory allows you to generate prospect activity, even if the building does not meet the initial needs of the prospective client. The Tennessee Valley Authority (TVA) lists 26 spec/quick turnaround buildings for their entire seven-state electric distribution area, for sale or lease on its website as of July 2020.

Beware; spec buildings do come with risks. We've seen spec buildings that are acquired when the foundation has been poured or when the steel is just going up. We've also seen one spec building sit on the market for seven years. It was a poorly designed building in a location with weak transportation access in a remote rural location; I wouldn't have placed a speculative building there. Recently I heard a panel speak from several national industrial real estate brokers that the average length of time a spec building sat vacant was two years. I believe that is more anecdotal than fact, but it's a good rule of thumb. If your community can invest and has a municipally owned industrial park, then it is my recommendation that the community find a way to develop a spec building.

Here is where leadership comes back into the discussion. Developing product takes financial and time resources, a plan, an execution strategy, and the fortitude to fend off the naysayers. It takes courage from leaders. The two (product and leadership) go hand in glove.

CHAPTER 3:

Market Regionally, Sell Locally

Key Takeaways:

1. Companies look at regions first because of the labor draw, then they focus on the real estate (local).

2. The transaction (site or building purchase or lease) is always local. Thus, the rationale for the chapter title.

3. Tourism is economic development. Tourism helps create and then identify a community's brand — for example, Asheville, North Carolina and Santa Fe, New Mexico.

When it comes to economic development, many people assume that a geography's success, whether it's a state, region, or community, is predicated on the success of a logo and tagline. Remember, "I Love New York"? Or "Virginia is for Lovers"? Those are memorable taglines. But did they help create economic success in those respective states? Debatable, of course. Regardless, communities of all sizes need to create a strong brand identity and promotional effort to support your economic development (wealth-building) efforts. You must raise awareness about the community both externally and within the local community with its local populous.

Typically, only larger communities have a budget that would make a difference in creating a brand and awareness. But economic development is always local. The transaction is local. So, working with a regional entity to promote a region can be valuable. Let's first discuss the value of regionalism as it relates to economic development and then narrow it down to the local level.

Why is regional collaboration important? Location decisions are based on regions first, followed by communities. It's all about the labor shed and typically companies are considering between a 30- and 45-minute drive-time in assessing the workforce for a region. In today's very tight labor market related to persons with skills, companies are finding a necessity to extend the labor shed they'll go to in hiring job candidates. Obviously, the longer the drive-time commute, the greater the chance for employee turnover, absenteeism, and tardiness. But in a full labor market, it's the new normal. We will return to a full labor market post-COVID, but it will take a few years. The point is that companies are always looking at a region's labor shed first and foremost.

And then you have the benefits of company investments on a regional level. Say there is an auto assembly plant 30 minutes from my community. Chances are that my community, despite being 30 minutes away from this auto plant, is reaping several indirect economic benefits, such as the location of auto suppliers, number of houses sold, population gains, and new and increased retail opportunities. Thus, the return on investment on a regional level is not disputed. But, at the end of the day, the transaction, meaning the acquisition of the real estate, whether it's a purchase or a lease is *always* local. So, you cannot supplant a regional economic development effort with a local one.

They work in tandem with each other. Thus, the phrase, *Market regionally, Sell locally.*

As a former economic development practitioner who ran multiple economic development offices (EDO), depending on the size of the community I represented, I always tried to hitch my wagon with a better funded, *effective* regional EDO, so we could position my smaller community under the umbrella of a geographic region. Examples of some of these larger regional groups that may represent both urban and rural locations include the Greater Phoenix Economic Council (GPEC), which serves over a dozen municipalities in Maricopa County, Arizona; Team NEO (Northeast Ohio), which serves the Cleveland, Akron, Canton, and Youngstown areas of Ohio; Florida's Great Northwest, which serves the Florida Panhandle; and the Kansas City Area Development Council, which serves multiple jurisdictions in both Missouri and Kansas.

If your community is smaller with limited resources for marketing and no regional group to help you, it is still incumbent on you to find a way to brand and market your community individually. This was one of several reasons the Texas miracle economic model was created in 1979 to decentralize economic development and allow communities to control their own destiny. Their vote on a half-cent sales tax for economic development purposes was then, and is still today, transformative. Branding and marketing are eligible expenses from sales tax monies. When I ran the Asheville, North Carolina, Chamber in the 1990s, I had to create our own marketing initiative since there was no regional group that could do it for our community effectively. But I did find the funds to do so, through a hotel room tax.

Why is it important to brand your community regionally and locally? Destination marketing organizations (tourism groups) and EDOs have successfully implemented the principle of branding to raise brand awareness of areas and market them cohesively. In a past webinar hosted by the media firm Atlas Integrated, it focused on the positive influence tourism can have on traditional economic development efforts. In summary:

- Places leave the most lasting impressions on people, whether they're deciding where a company stays or relocates or where they want to vacation.

- More and more, companies are seeking to locate where the workforce and talent are, and visitors tend to seek options for their next vacations based on information they glean from the internet. How a community's brand attracts and retains those audiences is the destination, talent attraction, and overall economic development challenge of the next 25 years.

- With a discernible and credible brand, communities can be more successful and sincere in having a real dialogue about the community's assets, differentiating factors, and authentic character.

My advice is to keep the brand real. Do not try to present your community as something it really is not. Years ago, when biotech was the economic development rage du jour, too many companies tried to sell themselves as being the potential next biotech capital of the world. Yet, out of 3,141 counties in the United States, only about a dozen are positioned to be effective in attracting or growing bio. When Amazon did its global HQ2 search, it had 238 submissions.[8] Many of these communities had zero chance of winning this project, yet they spent tens of thousands of dollars

[8] Elizabeth Weise, "Amazon HQ2 timeline: The winners are New York City and Arlington, Virginia," September 12, 2018, https://www.usatoday.com/story/tech/science/2018/09/12/timeline-amazons-search-hq-2-its-second-headquarters/1273275002/.

to submit proposals and created a sense of false expectations with their constituents. Sure, there was some benefit to submitting by bringing the community together as a team, but time and money could have been spent more judiciously on creating product (as noted in Chapter 2) rather than chasing an unrealistic dream. So, keep the brand real. Don't chase companies that aren't a realistic fit within your target markets.

If you have a county with multiple municipalities within that county, or a region with many counties and municipalities, work to create a unified brand. We did that in many of the locations I worked as an EDO leader: Mobile, Asheville, and Chattanooga. Team NEO has done that successfully with their Cleveland+ campaign. Richmond, Virginia, has also done it effectively with its Greater Richmond Partnership and marketing campaign. And a statewide effort by Michigan has been successful in marketing many of its individual regions or communities, whiles still keeping it aligned with the Pure Michigan campaign.

It really should not matter if you represent a large or small community, urban or rural. There are so many examples of communities of all shapes and sizes in all areas of the country that have created their own success. They did so through leadership and by creating the tools to achieve that success. Branding, marketing, and the execution of these tactics separate the winners. Market regionally if you can. But always keep selling locally.

CHAPTER 4:

Is Your Labor Force Work Ready?

Key Takeaways:

1. An unexpected event such as the COVID-19 pandemic, natural climatic disasters, and terrorist events (e.g., 9/11) can cause a complete short or mid-term pivot on anything related to the economy and, ultimately, employment.

2. In the long term, a changing age demographic in the United States means more emphasis on building the talent pipeline.

3. Academia and businesses must be partners (and on the same page) in developing the

talent pipeline to fill the skills demand of businesses.

An economic development organization's success is measured in job creation, retention, and investment; in short — wealth creation for a community's citizens. The number one differentiator between your community and your competition is having irrefutable proof of a skilled workforce that is ready to work *today*, as well as a talent pipeline that is ready to fill the jobs of *tomorrow*.

And then there's timing. I'm writing this chapter in late March 2020 during the greatest health and economic catastrophe of my lifetime — the coronavirus (COVID-19) pandemic. If I had written this chapter just two months earlier, I would have been touting the hottest economy in decades if not ever, the highest stock market gains ever with the Dow Jones Industrial Index nearing 30,000, the unemployment rate at full employment, hovering around 3%, and how nearly every employer you talk with representing nearly every type of business sector out there lamenting how challenging it was to find skilled, semi-skilled and lower-skilled individuals.

Then the virus hit. A black swan event like none other.[9]

This chapter will still focus on the fact that — even though the reset button has been hit and we will have double-digit unemployment rates for the short term — we will still see the demand for skilled talent in the long term and the challenges we face in filling the talent pipeline.

I'm calling this new recession we've entered "The Great Pause." Why? Because I'm predicting that within two years, and also depending on the outcome of the presidential and congressional elections, employment could come roaring back as well as the stock market financial indices. One thing is for sure: as a result of COVID-19, the supply chain will be completely restructured, and we'll see more regionalization of where companies expand their operations. Companies engaged in medical supplies, pharma, and specific types of consumer electronics will see a shift of manufacturing operations from China to primarily the USMCA countries (United States, Mexico, and Canada). This will

---

[9] A black swan is an unpredictable event that is beyond what is normally expected of a situation and has potentially severe consequences. Black swan events are characterized by their extreme rarity and their severe impact.

allow for the free movement of supplies, ingredients, and components to the United States and help prevent the shortages of medical supplies and certain types of pharmaceuticals experienced during the pandemic. With adversity comes opportunity, and I would tell economic development practitioners to work with your government officials and the business sector to be ready. Remember, *No product, No project*™. The pent-up demand to spend and grow the economy will be enormous.

I also believe the labor force participation rate (employed or actively seeking employment) could increase from a current US average of 63 percent to a high of 70 percent, based on financial losses to nearing retired or formerly retired workers and their savings plans. Thus, creating a larger pool in the workforce until the economy once again stabilizes. All of that said, we'll still have skilled labor shortages once all of this shakes out, so growing and sustaining the talent pipeline is still essential.

Call to Action

We've been hearing about the skills gap in the workplace for many years. The gap is real and it's growing — especially in technical jobs. What's happening to widen this gap? And what can be done to help reverse this situation?

There have been four industrial revolutions since the late 1700s, each brought about by innovation. The first was driven by mechanization and steam power, the second by electricity and mass production. The third began in the 1980s with computers and automation. And in 2013, America moved from the third industrial revolution to the fourth — known as I4 or Industry 4.0 — denoted by cyber-physical systems. The I4 drivers are artificial intelligence; big data analytics; and faster, smaller computing — all connecting and freely flowing in a high-tech, high-speed, and wireless cloud.

How Do We Fix This?

There's much work to be done to close the skills gap in the age of I4. The first step is recognizing there's not only a skills gap but a *technology* skills gap. The second step is ensuring that your community workforce development plan is centered on advancing technology skills for both the short- and long-term talent pipeline for its core clusters like manufacturing, logistics, healthcare, biotech, and others. Given the current workforce trend that as many workers will be over 40 as under, companies will have to ensure technology training is a core part of professional development for all workers. For the emerging workforce, community strategy needs to ensure the talent pipeline has a robust career navigation plan for students that includes technology skill development and tracking their STEM readiness at every node on their career trajectory. Third, the education system, from K–12 to postsecondary and lifelong learning, must integrate a robust technical learning experience for students and workers. Educators will need to challenge and encourage students of all ages to learn more about technology to advance their careers while helping their employers advance their bottom line.

What can communities do to ensure a quality labor force that meets the demand of your local employers? There's no one perfect recipe. To build the talent pipeline, many tactics need to be deployed. There are 13,500 public school districts in the United States, and they comprise 132,853 public K–12 schools, according to 2015–16 data from the National Center for Education Statistics (NCES). With this many schools and school districts, how do you ensure a level of education that the end user (businesses) need to employ those matriculating through K–12 schools? **Career pathways** is one of those tactics. It's a workforce development strategy used to support workers' transitions from education into the workforce. This strategy has been adopted at the federal, state, and local levels to increase education, training, and learning opportunities for America's current and emerging workforce. Many school districts utilize some form of career pathways or career academies. If deployed well, the design of the program takes into consideration the largest clusters of employment within that school district's region. So, you may see career pathways in healthcare, aerospace, coding, culinary arts, manufacturing, and more. To some, it's an early extension to technical or community college, and in fact, many high school students are dual-enrolled in both, thus allowing them to receive college credit before they even graduate high school. This dual enrollment is also called Early College.[10]

Another tactic used by a growing number of workforce development providers is high school **apprenticeships**. The US Department of Labor explains apprenticeships this way:

> *High school (HS) apprenticeship programs combine work-based, on-the-job learning*

---

[10] "What We Do: Early College," JFF, accessed July 11, 2020, https://www.jff.org/what-we-do/impact-stories/early-college/.

with relevant technical education in the classroom. Students who participate in these programs graduate with a high school diploma, earn college credits, and industry credentials. They also start on a career path that continues after high school graduation — whether that is a continuation of their apprenticeship along with college, college only, apprenticeship only, or other full-time employment. HS apprenticeships benefit businesses as well by providing a fresh source of talent developed from within their community.[11]

The Commonwealth of Kentucky has a best practice apprenticeships program they call "modern apprenticeship."[12] A modern apprenticeship is an employee training program that combines on-the-job training and classroom instruction under the supervision of an experienced industry professional. Other states and regions have also designed apprenticeships effectively to build the talent pipeline. Greensboro

---

[11] United States Department of Labor, "High School Apprenticeships: A Guide for Starting Successful Programs," https://www.apprenticeship.gov/sites/default/files/2019-04/HS_Apprenticeship_Youth_Guide_FINAL_2010831.pdf.

[12] "Apprenticeship: Where to Find Your Next Great Hire," Kentucky Education and Workforce Development Cabinet," accessed July 11, 2020, https://educationcabinet.ky.gov/Initiatives/apprenticeship/Pages/default.aspx.

(Guilford County), North Carolina, has an excellent example designed on the local level, named Guilford Apprenticeship Partners (GAP).[13] Apprentices can earn money on the job as soon as they start the apprenticeship program while also taking college classes at no cost.

Community and vocational colleges have been the unsung heroes for years in helping to build the talent pipeline, especially in those occupations that employ the skilled trades. For years, many parents and educators instilled a negative stigma on their children and students for attending a two-year college instead of a four-year college, or in receiving a certificate or credential for finishing a technical school. But with rising student debt and four-year graduates working barely above the minimum wage in some fields (primarily in the liberal arts), community and technical colleges are now seeing a strong enrollment with many graduates or completions finding economically viable employment upon graduation. Parents and educators need to embrace the value of vo-tech education. The alternative for many is student debt that saddles the graduate for years.

---

[13] Guilford Apprenticeship Partners, accessed July 11, 2020, https://gapnc.org/.

Some K–12 systems stand out as a best practice though, getting an early jump on capturing students while in high school and preparing them for the workforce just out of high school. One such example is the Southern Indiana Career and Technical Center, a product of the Evansville/Vanderburgh School Corporation.[14] This innovative center is the hub for the development and delivery of advanced career and technical education, workforce development, and training for the entire southwest Indiana region. High school students from five counties can receive classroom and hands-on training in 22 diverse areas of study, using the latest emerging technologies and equipment.

A final tactic to consider in building your talent pipeline is to hire the formerly incarcerated that have been trained at a technical college in prison, like Ingram State Technical College in Alabama.[15] The college is a fully accredited member of the Alabama Community College System. Established by the Alabama Legislature in 1965, this nationally recognized, award-winning college serves incarcerated students exclusively. Seventeen

[14] Southern Indiana Career and Technical College, accessed July 11, 2020, https://sictc.evscschools.com/.
[15] Ingram State Technical College, accessed July 11, 2020, https://istc.edu/

career technical programs, from automotive body repair to welding, make this institution and the graduates from this program highly popular with regional employers.

Labor shortages will see fluctuations of supply and demand in the age of COVID-19. But as long as the fundamentals of a strong economy are in place, long-term skill shortages will persist. Having business and academia on the same page is the recipe for success. That means academic institutions need to be adaptive and flexible to meet the demands of what businesses are seeing in today's and tomorrow's economic environment. Those states, regions, and communities that have embraced this public-private partnership are those who will be the winners in this very competitive global environment.

CHAPTER 5

Grow Your Garden

Key Takeaways:

1. Your existing businesses and entrepreneurs are your most important source of job creation leads.

2. Do not rely on one single employer or industry — diversify.

3. Incentives can be great tools to close important deals but educate yourself to prevent bad deals.

Once again, let's call to mind when Amazon announced they were seeking a location for a second headquarters and communities from across the country were catapulted into a frenzy, pledging huge incentive packages to attract Amazon to their community.

Every leader wants to land the "big fish" that will secure hundreds or thousands of jobs to their community, attract media attention, and bring the governor to town. However, this strategy is often as successful as playing the lottery and quickly attracts the scorn of your existing business community. The big fish are scarce and know how to play the game. Business attraction is certainly an important piece of your community's economic development strategy and must be pursued, but it should be balanced with the high growth potential that sits in your community's backyard from existing businesses and entrepreneurs.

Your community has already done the hard work to convince your existing businesses to expand or grow holistically in your city. They're already vested in your community and contributing to your tax base. Does that mean they're done growing or investing? Absolutely not. Existing businesses are an incredible source of business expansion leads and are some of your lowest hanging fruit. Understanding their specific needs will help you unlock their growth potential.

Similarly, entrepreneurs are the lifeblood of new ideas, technologies, businesses, and jobs in our communities. However, entrepreneurs need access to accelerators and incubators, venture and early-stage capital, infrastructure, information, advice, counsel, training, and peer networks to move their business ideas forward.[16] With the resources and support in place, entrepreneurs can quickly move from a 200-square-foot garage to becoming your community's most important employer. As such, growing your entrepreneurship ecosystem deserves your attention and continued community investment.

Business Retention

A key tenet of a community's economic development strategy is retaining and growing the businesses that exist within your community. A great place to start is by forming a Business Retention and Expansion (BR&E) program. Who

---

[16] An accelerator accelerates the growth of an existing startup and condenses multiple years' worth of business building into just a few months. Incubators incubate an idea so it can be eventually transformed into a business model. Incubators provide counselling and a shared workspace for flexible periods of time, one plus years. http://sehub.stanford.edu/accelerator-incubator; Venture capital are funds flowing into a company, generally during pre-IPO process, in the form of an investment rather than a loan. Controlled by an individual or small group known as venture capitalists, these investments require a high rate of return and are secured by a substantial ownership position in the business. https://www.entrepreneur.com/encyclopedia/venture-capital

are your largest employers? Which businesses are growing the fastest? Which are most likely to leave your community? What common challenges are businesses experiencing? These are important insights that you discover with a solid BR&E program. Existing businesses want to feel the love and know you still appreciate their investment and growth. Having your economic development staff schedule visits with a company's leadership reinforces that message while helping you to collect critical information about their plans and your business climate.

A solid business retention program should include annual or biennial visits that will help you anticipate closures and lease expirations or discover growth possibilities or other challenges and proactively address them. Maybe you learn that a business is experiencing a utility challenge that your staff can solve with a phone call or that the company is searching for a new 20,000-square-foot building after landing a couple of new contracts. While each visit will not always result in an expansion project, the on-the-ground feedback to your economic development staff will provide you, as a community leader, critical insights into your community's business climate and challenges as well as areas where policymakers need to find solutions.

Similar to diversifying one's retirement account to mitigate investment risk, a solid business retention program also reduces risk during recessions. Companies get bought out, economic conditions fluctuate, technologies change, and a big incentive offer makes it easy for companies to relocate. When the Great Recession hit (2008–2009), the most resilient cities were the ones that had a diverse collection of industries that weathered the storm differently. Your community needs to diversify your local economic base to ensure that your community can weather recessions and have different businesses growing in different seasons. You certainly don't want your community's economic health to rely on one specific employer and risk a disaster down the road when they move or close. A good defense is sometimes the best offense.

Recognizing your businesses and stakeholders that are critical to your economic development success requires constant attention. A handwritten note is one of the easiest and cheapest ways to thank your top businesses and investors each year. My office always does this after each BR&E visit and around the holidays. This gesture reminds businesses that you're there to serve them anytime they need anything. A business recognition program is another nice touch to acknowledge long-time businesses. Some turn this into an evening event where awards are not only handed out for businesses celebrating their 5–100+-year anniversaries, but also for categories such as the most innovative new business, fastest-growing, or philanthropic giving. That said, your gesture doesn't need to be that extravagant. Businesses simply want to know that you're their partner and appreciate them.

Entrepreneurship

Today, entrepreneurs can work from anywhere. However, they also need infrastructure (including Wi-Fi and amenities), affordable living, and access to capital to move their business ideas forward. Similar to the one-stop shop concept we discussed in Chapter 1, your community should have a dedicated entrepreneurship center that can direct entrepreneurs to the resources, capital, and information that fit their unique needs. This office can include representatives and resources from your local university, extension office, small business development center (SBDC), incubators and accelerators, and advocates/peer networks. This will require strong leadership and public-private partnerships, but the long-term investment pays off. Rawlins, Wyoming, is a great example of a rural community that was successful at establishing this resource on its main street and has seen significant revitalization from its initial investment. Chattanooga, Tennessee, is a great example of a city implementing a long-term entrepreneurship strategy that allowed them to become one of the first "gig cities" in the United States and has helped them both start and attract countless tech-based companies.

Remember the mantra that *Talent is the new currency*? Some cities complement their budding entrepreneurship scene by encouraging remote workers to relocate to their community. These communities often are trying to combat population loss or brain drain by incentivizing individuals who already have full-time employment elsewhere or are self-employed in another city and have the flexibility to work from anywhere.[17] Communities offer incentives ranging from cash incentives to down-payment assistance to student loan

---

[17] Brain drain is the relocation and loss of highly trained or intelligent people from a particular community.

forgiveness and free rent and coworking space. An innovative model can be found in Burlington, Vermont,[18] but there are communities across the country that are incorporating this strategy to build upon their established cadre of entrepreneurs and retain a skilled, innovative workforce.[19] Ultimately, this effort increases their talent pool and creates opportunities down the road.

Entrepreneurship also does not exclusively mean high-tech. Entrepreneurs that wish to open up their own wine bar, salon, gym, coffee shop, hardware store, or plumbing business on Main Street are just as important as those entrepreneurs developing apps and software. Technology is used by every business. Importantly, many owners of our Main Street businesses are nearing retirement and looking for the next generation to purchase their business. Preparing entrepreneurs to run these businesses and helping connect them with business owners looking to sell is an excellent opportunity for every community over the next decade.

---

[18] Dan D'Ambrosio, "Is Vermont's $10,000 Incentive Program for Remote Workers Working? It Depends Who You Ask," November 19, 2019, https://www.burlingtonfreepress.com/story/money/2019/11/19/vermonts-10-000-pay-move-remote-worker-program-does-work/4189358002/.

[19] Glassdoor Team, "Cities & States That Will Pay You to Move There," July 17, 2019, https://www.glassdoor.com/blog/cities-states-that-will-pay-you-to-move-there/.

Incentives

Now, let's talk about incentives. Few things attract the ire of people and media attention in my profession as much as incentives. Incentives certainly have a dark side and some communities throw out incentives without a second thought. I want to change this dynamic.

Incentives are an important tool when used intelligently and are necessary due to the inherent competition between localities for new businesses, new investments, and jobs. That said, incentives should be used prudently on projects where they'll be a deciding factor on whether a business will either remain or locate in a community, ensuring that it creates a win-win for both the community and investor. In short, incentives are public investments to achieve public policy goals. Each deal should have clear community or fiscal benefits that are well documented, analyzed, and communicated to citizens so everyone understands how the public will benefit from the initial investment. Remember, incentives don't make a bad site or an inferior community good. What they really do is close the deal.

I recommend scheduling a day-long onboarding meeting with your local economic development team to understand every incentive tool that you have available, what it is, how it works, and how it fits into your community's economic development strategy. Different incentives accomplish different policy goals. While a payroll incentive is always used to attract or expand companies that bring investment and jobs, a community's property tax abatement program may be targeted toward increasing a community's inventory of affordable housing or to encourage more sustainable development. Tax increment financing (TIF) incentives are generally focused on large-scale public infrastructure, but they can be used for other creative uses as well. Other tools, such as Industrial Revenue Bonds (IRB), forgo some of the property taxes to attract the more lucrative payroll taxes.

You need to understand how each incentive is aligned with your economic development strategy and how each is structured to close a financial gap in a deal. Tools have different terms and structures. Some are a direct capital investment by a community at the start of the deal, while others are annual incentives that can last up to 40 years!

Incentives are often misunderstood, and because they're complicated, other parties can easily take advantage of them or cause your community to make poor deals. You must educate yourself and ensure each deal will deliver a strong return on investment for the public. Used intelligently, incentives can be a powerful force to closing deals that will attract new investment, jobs, and revitalization to your community, all of which can be backed up with performance commitments from the other party and incentive underwriting. However, if you do not take the time to understand your tools and analyze each project's cost/benefits, your community will be outsmarted and risk your reputation being tied to poor deals.

After you're educated on your tools and how they're being used, you need to constantly reassess your policies to make sure they're being used effectively. Here are some best practice tips for an incentive policy:

- **Focus on primary or value-added jobs.** A primary job is one that produces goods and/or services for customers that are predominately outside of the community. This creates new "outside" dollars for the community.

- **Require an incentive application**. You need to document what each applicant will bring to the table and then analyze and underwrite the project to ensure the public receives a strong return on investment. Application fees are an expected cost of doing business.

- **Ensure projections are achievable and underwrite conservatively.** If the project performs better than anticipated, that's fantastic. But nobody wants the opposite.

- **Be cautious with offering long incentive terms on real estate incentives.** Incentives become less valuable over time and don't add much to a project's gap past year 15 or 20. You generally seek to frontload the incentive, then wean it off as the years progress. The same advice goes for payroll incentives. My office requires businesses remain in Covington for twice the incentivized period, ensuring we receive a strong ROI for our taxpayers.

- **Every deal is different.** While there needs to be parameters so developers and businesses have a general framework of your incentive terms, every incentive should not have the same deal terms as the last and handed out like candy! Each project has different advantages to the community and different financial gap needs.

- **Create performance agreements.** Agreements should have clawbacks if businesses or developers don't meet their obligations. If one side isn't performing, you need to reassess and take action.

- **Track performance.** If you aren't tracking performance, then you will never be able to improve your policies or understand whether incentives are truly working toward your economic development goals.

- **You don't know what you don't know!** The National Development Council is a national nonprofit community development organization that works with local, state, and community organizations. They are an excellent resource for communities looking for assistance when structuring challenging real estate developments or programs, but also provide low-cost training to help communities negotiate better deals.

While there are successful communities with well-established incentive programs, another community to check out is Littleton, Colorado. After losing some of its top businesses, its city leadership and economic development staff froze its incentive programs and focused on unlocking the growth potential of its existing businesses by using market data, marketing, and customized research. It was a stark departure from traditional thinking. Rather than simply offering incentives, it invested its economic development resources into developing research tools and targeted lead platforms that would help existing companies find new markets to unlock its growth potential. This provided businesses with critical insights that helped make real-life business decisions. It was a longer-term approach that attracted its fair share of critics, but the community stuck with it and added 15,000 jobs without the use of incentives.[20] Today, Littleton stands as a model of the economic gardening approach by focusing on growing second-stage, high-growth businesses.

It's important to note that there's no one-size-fits-all approach. What works in one community may not work in another. There are excellent

---

[20] "Economic Gardening," Ewing Marion Kauffman Foundation, September 27, 2013, https://www.kauffman.org/resources/policy/economic-gardening/.

models from across the country that communities have implemented based on their specific community needs and market. I encourage you to contact others and not reinvent the wheel. Most communities are more than happy to share their best practices. Of course, your community will need to adjust for your specific market and laws, then continually improve upon your plan based on feedback from the business community. By doing all of this, your community will grow your garden and always have a pool of project leads in your back pocket.

CHAPTER 6
Time Kills Deals

Key Takeaways:

1. Government is often the great bottleneck of investment.

2. Regulations are important, but they must be continually improved and reassessed.

3. Strong customer service is crucial to keep the momentum going.

Covington, Kentucky, could not have been more excited about our new business prospect and the timing was perfect. We'd just elected a new mayor and our city commission was laser-focused on growing jobs and investment in the community.

ROAD iD was a cool, young company that sought the urban amenities, access, and talent that Covington offered. I knew that ROAD iD could become the poster child to kick off many of our new initiatives.

ROAD iD quickly fell in love with a historic, underutilized warehouse in the center of town and had the desire to turn this eyesore into its long-term home. To add to the street vibrancy, ROAD iD also wanted a coffee shop or restaurant on the first floor as an amenity for its employees and the community. I was thrilled. We had a company that was seeking to invest $4.2 million to restore a historic warehouse, land 72 new jobs and a headquarters facility in our community, and bring much-needed payroll tax revenue to the city.

Unfortunately, we got in our own way at every step of the process. Our zoning code didn't allow for a mixed-use development with both an office and restaurant in our manufacturing zone. Our antiquated zoning code didn't anticipate the blurred definition of ROAD iD's business model. Were they primarily manufacturing? Or were they an office use with limited manufacturing? Thus, ROAD iD had to work with our zoning staff, pay a zoning review fee, and ultimately plead its case before our zoning board at its monthly meeting.

ROAD iD's dream building also sat within our Historic Preservation Overlay. Since it intended to renovate the building's exterior, ROAD iD had to work with a different staff member and board. As ROAD iD conducted additional due diligence, a financial gap widened and we now needed to offer financial incentives to make the deal feasible. Add another staff member and another board. Oh, you want to close that alley, too? Please contact our Public Works Department. Need parking? Please contact the Parking Authority Board.

Ultimately, we closed the deal and the building turned out beautifully. ROAD iD has added to Covington's vibrancy and has become a huge cheerleader for our city's revitalization. That said, the project taught us that we had to get our own internal house in order to prevent other companies and investors from having to go through similar headaches and time delays.

It ain't sexy, but if you want to make a huge impact on your city's day-to-day business climate, start by cleaning up your internal procedures, administrative forms, and timelines. This is your first and last impression with most businesses and investors. These details often make or break whether someone will ever do another project in your city again. In a world where your community is competing for talent and investment, your city must move at the speed of business. If you don't, you'll lose the deal every time. Time kills deals.

Short-Term Steps

Pay attention to your office culture — Your staff are the face of your city. As any business knows, customer service is incredibly important. After an election, many staff in leadership positions step down or seek other opportunities while the newly elected leaders bring in fresh talent to implement their vision. Change is inevitable and necessary to reach your community's goals. Nevertheless, it's important to pay attention to the office culture during transitions. Transitions can be demoralizing and filled with uncertainty for staff. More importantly, if that becomes the office culture, it will permeate your staff's customer service to citizens and investors. Transitions and vacancies cause things to fall through the cracks and double a staff workload that's already stretched thin. Be transparent, communicative, and organize events to boost staff morale. It may sound small, but it will make a huge difference.

Look at your forms — If your applications, licenses, and other documents are called a Form

132b and look like they were last edited in 1962 (and they probably were), then it's time to get your internal house in order! Regulations are important, but remember, speed to market is the name of the game. Permits should not take months to be approved. Put yourself in the shoes of an investor and identify every step in their approval process. You might be shocked. Do your forms make sense to the average person or even to the staff processing them? Can one application serve the role that two are currently serving? Can it be submitted online with digital attachments rather than in person? How long does an application take to receive feedback or be approved? Start finding every touchpoint and fixing the inevitable inefficiencies that have happened over time. This is a simple change that can shave days (even weeks) off a project's timeline.

New business guide — Most people have no idea where to start when interacting with their local government. That's why creating a new business guide was one of the first things I did when I arrived in Covington. This simple document is a checklist that shows entrepreneurs every step necessary to open for business and provides useful tips and staff contact information. I cannot tell you how many people thanked me for creating this simple document.

Predevelopment meeting — No investor wants to discover costly surprises that could have easily been remedied at the beginning if all parties had communicated better or asked the right questions. Many projects have complex development questions that inevitably involve many departments. Be proactive and coordinate a predevelopment meeting with businesses or developers to discuss proposals. Make sure you have knowledgeable department representatives who can answer questions or creatively address solutions to each challenge. We have zoning, building permits, economic development, and solid waste at every meeting, then invite other departments as necessary. If you have enough demand, you can even hold "office hours" where prospective businesses or developers can walk in and ask questions about their proposal to save time and money. Encouraging regular predevelopment meetings is an easy customer-friendly practice that can address small problems before they become deal-killers.

Long-Term Steps

One-stop shop/ombudsman — Your community should aim to create a one-stop shop to facilitate the zoning, planning, and inspections process. The permitting process is an intimidating experience for any applicant. A one-stop shop helps those who live or do business in your community find what they need in the most efficient, time-saving manner. Information on your community's development processes, including case submittals, plan submittals, permits, and development records, would be accessible in one location. Whether a business is looking to develop a property or renovate a commercial building, this one-stop shop would be the place to start. In addition, creating an ombudsman or concierge staffing position is an excellent way to serve as customer's main point of contact and find solutions throughout the permitting process. Both are customer-focused initiatives that will help any community transform into a leader in effective service delivery. As we mentioned in Chapter 1, the cities of El Paso, Texas, or Scottsdale, Arizona, are great examples.

Form-based code — Our historic properties are often found in our main streets and house many of our mom-and-pop businesses. Unfortunately, many of our community's historic properties are vacant, blighted, and struggling to survive. There are abundant reasons for this, but one of the culprits could be your community's zoning and building codes. Often, our zoning and building codes were adopted much later and rarely designed for historic properties, inevitably causing historic properties to be burdened with bureaucratic red tape and additional fees that ward off potential investors. Unlike traditional zoning codes, form-based code focuses on how the building addresses the street, rather than on who the end user will be. Form-based code streamlines permits, allows flexibility when redeveloping historic properties, and allows the market to dictate what goes into a space. We didn't have a form-based code in place for ROAD iD, but we learned our lesson and will be adopting a form-based code soon. There are many communities that have moved to a form-based code, but Lafayette, Louisiana, is a great model.[21] It won the 2019 Driehaus Form-Based Codes Award for its simple, short, and illustrated model designed for investors.

---

[21] https://www.downtownlafayette.org/resources/downtown-action-plan/

Historic building code — Similarly, our building codes can be burdensome and deter investment. Like many in my field, I recommend adopting a rehabilitation code based on the New Jersey Rehabilitation Subcode.[22] New Jersey has been able to cut rehabilitation costs by 50% and make it financially feasible to renovate its historic building stock, driving investment and business back to historic business districts.

Too many boards — Many communities have an appointed board for everything, and the same project may need approval from two to three different boards. These boards can add significant delays to a project. Can you save time and find ways to address most issues administratively, saving the most complicated cases for board review? Are there ways to combine boards to review the entire project at once, rather than piecemeal? This may take time, but it will help loosen the investment bottleneck. Again, it ain't sexy, but it's all about speed to market. Don't forget, time kills deals.

---

[22] "Rehabilitation Subcode," State of New Jersey Department of Consumer Affairs, accessed July 11, 2020,
https://www.nj.gov/dca/divisions/codes/offices/rehab.html.

CHAPTER 7:

It's All About the Brand

Key Takeaways:

1. Your brand is the foundation of your larger economic development efforts.

2. Celebrate every win — no matter how big or small.

3. Every event is your opportunity to shine.

4. Ensure someone is focused on the day-to-day health and vibrancy of your business districts.

Our town squares, business districts, or downtowns used to be the heartbeat of our communities, and it's critically important to reactivate them. Investing in placemaking may not seem like a traditional economic development investment, but it creates the buzz and branding necessary to attract future investment. Remember, you must sell locally. Your community is competing against countless other communities for businesses, residents, talent, and investment. If you're going to be successful in your larger economic development efforts, you need to constantly market your brand, programs, and your successes to keep the momentum going and attract more residents and businesses to your community.

Back in October 2019, I decided to ride 156 miles on a bike trail near me that travels through urban cities, small towns, countryside, and wooded parks. On this journey, I discovered the charm and long-term strategic placemaking investments by the two small communities of Loveland (population 12,700) and Yellow Springs, Ohio (population 3,700). If you visit Loveland, the bike path runs straight through the center of the town and is packed with bicyclists, dog walkers, and baby strollers. It is the heartbeat of the community and runs directly past a bike shop, brewery, restaurants, and many other neighborhood businesses. Visitors flood in for relaxing bike rides and entertainment, while residents stay to enjoy the amenities throughout the year. Despite only being located on a small portion of the much larger 78-mile trail, most people in Cincinnati recognize it as the "Loveland Bike Trail" and have no idea that its formal name is the Little Miami Bike Trail. The town branded itself around the asset and continually invests in that brand. The result has helped Loveland land several new employers and housing developments to their community.

Meanwhile, Yellow Springs is a progressive, hippie gem of a community that leverages the same asset differently, but amazingly well. Foot traffic from the trail has helped the town attract amazing independent restaurants, an excellent brewery, and artistic shops surrounding the bike path. Whereas other Main Streets are struggling, Yellow Spring's vacancies are few and the district is consistently activated with art and music designed to entice tourists from the trail and make the city welcoming and memorable.

What is your community's charm factor? Or, what is your weirdness factor? Some communities brand themselves around music and art while others embrace fitness, food, beer, or bourbon. Your commercial offerings can reinforce your brand and provide the unique experiences that emphasize the character of your community. I've added several recommendations below to get started, but the possibilities are endless. Government should not be the face of the effort, but it may critical to setting up a sustainable framework. Activating and marketing your community with events and investments throughout the year is the building block for your larger economic development efforts. It's all about the brand.

Short-Term Steps

Focus on cleanliness and safety — If your town center or business district is struggling with perceptions of cleanliness or safety, this must be addressed first. Perception is reality and no one will want to invest where there is perceived crime and blight. Walnut Hills is a neighborhood of Cincinnati that had long-struggled with disinvestment and high vacancy. A few years ago, the Walnut Hill Community Urban Redevelopment Foundation placed some milk crates around a keg of beer and invited neighbors for a weekly outdoor happy hour on a street corner that struggled with negative perceptions of cleanliness and safety. The grassroots idea took off, and they started attracting a crowd each week. That keg changed perceptions and became the building block to kick off many other real estate projects. It allowed the neighborhood to build its product and brand to attract new residents and talent. In 2020, Walnut Hills will be welcoming Cincinnati's first Black-owned brewery to the neighborhood right across the street from the original community event,[23] and the neighborhood continues to attract new creative office users, shops, and residents.

Start a rent and facade program — When I started working in Covington, our business districts and nodes struggled with high vacancies and a "tired, worn-down" appearance. With a budget of $36,000, we implemented a competitive Rent Subsidy and Facade Improvement Program to assist six businesses. The Rent Subsidy program offers new businesses up to $500 off their rent for one year if they sign a two-year lease. The facade program provides a 50/50 match, up to $6,000, to enhance the property's (and district's) appearance. The program has been wildly successful. We

---

[23] Garin Pirnia, "Esoteric Brewing, Cincinnati's First Minority-Owned Brewery, is Slated to Open in Walnut Hills This May," City Beat, February 18, 2020, https://www.citybeat.com/food-drink/whats-the-hops/article/21116773/esoteric-brewing-cincinnatis-first-minorityowned-brewery-is-slated-to-open-in-walnut-hills-this-may.

started with $36,000 and ran out in six months. We doubled it the next year and ran out in six months. We now have an annual budget of $150,000 and still run out each year. This simple program has filled countless vacancies in Covington with exciting new neighborhood businesses, while enhancing over 50 properties to spruce up our "curb appeal." The program is both a business attraction and business retention incentive. If your community is struggling with similar challenges, a $6,000 incentive can go a long way, and the money makes a huge difference to the bottom line for small businesses.

Start a community development corporation or Main Street organization — Having an organization that is responsible for the day-to-day health and vibrancy of your community's business district is incredibly important. Think about a mall. The operators are always striving to ensure the facility is clean, attractive, and filled with the right mix of businesses that will attract customers and make the experience memorable and enjoyable. Your community needs an entity that acts the same way. Unfortunately, many communities struggle with commercial vacancies and deteriorating buildings in their business districts. Landlords are often more motivated to find *a* tenant than finding the *right* tenant. I'm a huge proponent of partnering with an organization that can purchase and redevelop the "worst of the worst" properties, find the right commercial tenants, and program them effectively to reactivate your business district. These efforts can be costly and time-consuming, but getting control of your most challenging properties and having someone focused on attracting the right tenants are critical to the health of your business district and your larger economic development goals. The entity that controls the dirt controls the project. There are great examples across the country, but I have always been impressed with College Hill Community Urban Redevelopment Corporation in Cincinnati.[24]

Fill with programming — Activating your business districts requires programming to attract foot traffic. This doesn't need to be expensive or costly. Burlington, Vermont, found an effective, cost-friendly solution by "hiring" highly skilled street performers on Church Street that provide entertainment while people shop and dine.[25] These performers mostly work for tips. It was such a

[24] College Hill Community Urban Redevelopment Corporation, accessed July 11, 2020, https://chcurc.com/.
[25] "Street Performers," Church Street Marketplace, accessed July 11, 2020, https://www.churchstmarketplace.com/information/street-performers.

simple and cheap way to make the community and retail district pop and differentiate Burlington from nearby communities. Find similar ways to program your commercial corridors to reinforce your brand and make the customer experience and neighborhood memorable.

Hire a special events manager/ombudsman — Big events drive foot traffic and excitement to your community. They also reinforce your community's brand and are your community's opportunity to shine. When residents or guests arrive, will they be frantically searching for available parking, or will there be a flagger directing guests to park in your community's parking lot (ahem, revenue opportunity!) with regular shuttles to the event? Will trash cans be overflowing because they were an afterthought, or will there be plenty of trash and recycling receptacles with regular pickups? Will the event need a street closure, police presence, or alcohol license? Hire someone who can ensure your community shines at these events, and it will help every other aspect of your community's brand, relations with existing business, and future prospects.

Celebrate every win — Finally, it is imperative that people recognize the projects and excitement that you're building in your community. You need to be the community cheerleader. Internally, it is imperative that you ensure that your residents are aware of the exciting projects in the neighborhood and realize how the investment will impact them. Externally, it's important to promote your successes and constantly use them to market your brand to attract new businesses, talent, residents, and tourists. Keep investing in the message. Educate everyone on how the project is a win for them and matters to the community. And be sure to celebrate the small deals just as much as the large deals. Every business and resident you meet is a new prospect and opportunity. Be sure to ask businesses whether they've considered moving to your community, and be ready to talk about the advantages your community can offer them. Make sure all your colleagues are doing the same. Economic development is very relationship-based. I've seen community leaders start several business deals from that exact scenario.

CHAPTER 8

Control Your Own Destiny or Someone Else Will

Key Takeaways:

1. Work in collaboration, but don't solely rely on others to shape the destiny of your community.

2. A crisis is typically a catalyst for change.

3. With adversity comes opportunity.

4. Lead, follow, or get out of the way.

Legendary business icon Jack Welch, former chairman of GE, once said, "Control your own destiny or someone else will." What does that mean? If you're an elected or appointed official relying on federal, state, or local governments to solve your community's problems, make your community competitive, and win in the economic development arena, then chances are you're going to be left behind.

I admire and congratulate the leaders who've dared to take control of their environment. Earlier in this book, I used and discussed what I call the "Texas economic miracle" from the legislative approval in 1979 of a half-cent sales tax for economic development, or as the Texas comptroller calls it, "Developing Industries & Cultivating Communities." Remember Chapter 2? *No product, No project*™. You must have product to successfully create wealth-building in a community. The Texas legislature basically told local communities that they, local government, can do a better job if they have the resources to execute economic development more effectively than if the state tells them how to do it. In essence, the legislature told these local communities, You folks need to control your own destiny, and we'll give you the resources that allow you to do so — a win-

win for everyone involved. But Texas is just one example of effective leadership controlling their own destiny. The transformation of Chattanooga, Tennessee, and Greenville, South Carolina, are great examples of local communities controlling their own destiny.

Greenville has become a renowned success story of downtown revitalization.[26] Like many struggling urban cores in the 1960s and '70s, the leadership of Greenville recognized that change needed to occur. Leaders commissioned a downtown plan in 1968, implemented the plan in the 1970s with new product that would help anchor and catalyze additional investment, in this case a performing arts center (Peace Center), and continued to help nurture product with streetscapes, hotels, a larger arena (Bi-Lo Center), and a baseball stadium (Fluor Field). Product helped attract investment, including Michelin to Greenville. BMW located in neighboring Spartanburg, but with a tremendous regional return on investment that impacts Greenville. Three downtown TIF districts provided key funding for

[26] "Downtown Reborn," City of Greenville, South Carolina, accessed July 11, 2020, https://citygis.greenvillesc.gov/downtownreborn/index.html.

numerous streetscapes, parking, and infrastructure improvements to support private development. Residential is growing exponentially.

Today, downtown Greenville gets 2.5 million visitors annually. The leaders of the community never gave up. They created a plan, worked it effectively, updated it as they checked off successes, and adjusted to changes in consumer preferences. Most important, they kept nurturing and attracting new leadership. They did not rely on others to create their success; they created their own success.

Chattanooga is different. Concern by community leaders about the long-term future of the community served as the catalyst for change. There was a sense of urgency. In 1969, the federal EPA declared that Chattanooga had the dirtiest air in the nation.[27] By the mid-1980s, local leaders launched Vision 2000, an effort to revitalize and reinvent Chattanooga's culture and economy. This included early efforts in the concept of sustainability where the environment, economy, and culture work in tandem with one another.[28]

---

[27] Greg Beach, "How America's Dirtiest City in 1969 Became One of the Greenest," Inhabitat, August 19, 2016, https://inhabitat.com/how-americas-dirtiest-city-in-1969-became-one-of-the-greenest/.

[28] Mitchell Grant, "Sustainability" Investopedia, April 5, 2020, https://www.investopedia.com/terms/s/sustainability.asp.

Chattanooga's population declined by more than 10 percent in the 1980s but regained it over the next two decades — the only major US city to do so. The Tennessee Aquarium opened in 1992, setting the stage for downtown Chattanooga's early renaissance. The Creative Discovery Museum opened in 1995, again helping to set the stage for hotel developments and other quality of place attractions. In 2002, then-Mayor Bob Corker, who later became a US senator, wanted to kick-start more investment in the community and served as the visionary and impetus behind the "21st Century Waterfront Plan" — a $120 million redevelopment of the Chattanooga waterfront area, which was completed in 2005. The city has won three national awards for outstanding "livability" and nine Gunther Blue Ribbon Awards for excellence in housing and consolidated planning.

In 2010, the Electric Power Board (EPB), the city-owned electric utility, became the first municipally owned utilities company in the United States to offer internet access directly to the public at speeds up to 10 gigabits (10,000 megabits) per second. The network has been emulated by at least six other cities in Tennessee and studied by other cities in the United States and internationally.

Many economic development pundits attribute the city's success in attracting Volkswagen's automobile assembly plant expansion and the location of Amazon's distribution facility to the region to these internet speeds.

According to city leaders, since the opening of the aquarium, downtown Chattanooga has received over $5 billion of private investment, including nearly $1 billion from 2014 to 2018. Private capital, philanthropic foundation support, and public dollars all helped to create the Chattanooga success story. It controlled its own destiny when a crisis developed. It created the tools and tactics to achieve success. Leadership — both public and private — made it happen.

If you're a community leader serving as an elected official, an appointed leader to help shape policy, a high-level volunteer to help guide policy, or staff leadership employed to execute policy, controlling your own destiny is an absolute must in the recipe for economic success. These successful communities implemented many of the steps we outlined in this book, and they can be modified in your community. Economic development is a constant investment — in building product, talent, businesses, and branding.

Your community cannot sell from an empty cart, so make sure you have the product that businesses want. Leverage the marketing resources of regions to build your pipeline of leads. But remember that the transaction is always local, and you cannot simply sit on the sidelines and hope others will close the deal.

Your community's talent pipeline is what businesses need to succeed, so be sure to create the successful partnerships to ensure that students are well-prepared. Continue to build your pipeline of leads in your own backyard from entrepreneurship and existing businesses, while simultaneously getting your own house in order to facilitate investment. And remember, you must continually invest in your brand.

Finally, since this book is designed to guide and assist leaders who aren't professional economic developers — and this isn't your day job — thank you for what you do. If you're a policymaker as an elected official or a board member for a chamber of commerce or economic development organization, you have one of the most important roles that can determine the winners and losers for economic development success. Poor leaders drive economic development out. Good leaders drive economic development to their respective geographies.

Be a good leader and transform your communities!

Acknowledgments

We sincerely appreciate you taking the time to read our book. We hope it leads your community or region on the path toward long-term economic success. We are fortunate to have the opportunity to work with leaders and communities across the country and to be part of their positive change. As such, we would love to hear from you!

If you found this book helpful, would you please leave us a review? Your review provides us with critical feedback to improve and helps us reach more community leaders down the road.

Should your community ever need more personalized assistance, such as industry targeting, strategic action plans, or advisory services, we would be thrilled to work with you.

You can also learn more about Garner Economics at
www.garnereconomics.com.

Finally, this book would not have been possible without the invaluable support and advice from Jason Reiner and Tom West, amazing editorial assistance from Kim Ledgerwood, and book publicity by Platinum PR.

About the Authors

Jay Garner is the president and founder of Garner Economics, LLC, an economic development and site location consulting firm headquartered in Atlanta, Georgia. He never really considered himself an author, though in his 40-year career, he has written dozens of articles and research papers for many different publications. He's applied his years of leading award-winning economic development organizations in places like Asheville, North Carolina; Mobile, Alabama; and Chattanooga, Tennessee, along with his seventeen plus years of leading his advisory practice to this book. When Ross Patten called Jay about this idea of writing a help book for economic development policy leaders, Jay listened since reaching that audience has been a passion of his for four decades. When he's not writing a book or making a living running his business, he's involved with his other passion of playing drums in a big band jazz orchestra. When asked which is more difficult, writing a book or playing drums, his reply was the typical response of economic developers, "It depends."

Ross Patten is the city of Covington, Kentucky's economic development project manager, and he focuses on business attraction, incentives, real estate development, business district revitalization, and entrepreneurism. His project list includes corporate relocations, large multifamily developments, infrastructure improvements, policy development, and countless small business and neighborhood enhancement projects. He was awarded City Hall Employee of the Year in 2017 and currently serves as the chair of the Advisory Board for Kentucky's Small Business Development Center. Ross has been recognized by Cincinnati's WCPO as a "Next Nine" Young Leaders to Watch. Ross spends his free time attempting to bake and investing in real estate. He lives in Cincinnati.

Made in the USA
Monee, IL
20 June 2021

71841914R00056